W9-CME-288

# HOW TO LIVE LIKE
# A MEDIEVAL
# KNIGHT

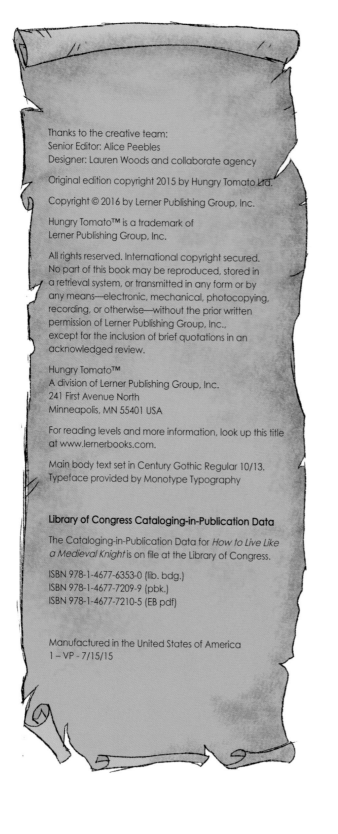

Thanks to the creative team:
Senior Editor: Alice Peebles
Designer: Lauren Woods and collaborate agency

Hungry Tomato™
A division of Lerner Publishing Group, Inc.
241 First Avenue North
Minneapolis, MN 55401 USA

For reading levels and more information, look up this title
at www.lernerbooks.com.

Main body text set in Century Gothic Regular 10/13.
Typeface provided by Monotype Typography

**Library of Congress Cataloging-in-Publication Data**

The Cataloging-in-Publication Data for *How to Live Like
a Medieval Knight* is on file at the Library of Congress.

ISBN 978-1-4677-6353-0 (lib. bdg.)
ISBN 978-1-4677-7209-9 (pbk.)
ISBN 978-1-4677-7210-5 (EB pdf)

Manufactured in the United States of America
1 – VP - 7/15/15

# HOW TO LIVE LIKE A MEDIEVAL KNIGHT

By Anita Ganeri

Illustrated by Mariano Epelbaum

HUNGRY TOMATO™

Minneapolis

# Contents

# Medieval Knight

It's the fourteenth century, and you've traveled back in time to the leafy town of Corfield in medieval England. I am Gilbert Marshall—squire in the service of my local lord, the Earl of Corfield. I've lived here since I was a page. Anyway, my training's nearly finished and it'll soon be time to go off to war. Wish me luck!

## What were the Middle Ages?

The Middle Ages, also called medieval times, were a period of history in Europe. The period lasted from the fall of the Roman Empire around the year 500 to the start of the **Renaissance** around 1300.

Life in the Middle Ages depends on your place in society. You're either free or unfree. Free people are lords, knights, commoners (merchants, craftsmen, and wage laborers), and freeholders (peasant farmers who own their own farms).The unfree are serfs (peasant farmers who do not own their land but work for their lord).

Pope / Church

Monarch

Knights

Lords

Merchants

Craftsmen

Free-holders

Serfs

Wage laborers

## Knights

Highly trained cavalrymen who fight for the king and barons in return for land

## Lords

Rule large areas of land for the king and pledge their loyalty and lives to him

## Monarch

Holds surpreme power in his own lands and often battles with other rulers

## Pope

Head of the Catholic Church in Rome, and also controls land and has huge political power

## Serfs

Lowest and largest class of people, who work a lord's land and are owned by him

## Wage laborers

Anyone who doesn't own land, but works land for other people for a day's wages

## Merchants

Travel far and wide to buy unusual or exotic goods that they trade at markets and fairs

## Freeholders

Peasant farmers who own their own land and farms and pay taxes to the king

## Craftsmen

Blacksmiths, stone masons, carpenters, and other skilled workers, who team up to form groups called guilds

# Knight in Training

Being a knight is something you inherit. My dad was a knight, too. And it's all I ever wanted to be. When I was little, I used to spend hours riding on my hobby horse and spearing things with my toy lance.

When I was seven, my dad sent me away from home to live in the Earl of Corfield's household as a **page**. There wasn't time to feel homesick—I was too busy learning to ride a horse, fight with a sword, and read and write. At fourteen years old, I was ready to become a **squire** for another seven years.

**WARNING!**

You have to practice hitting the target with a wooden lance at first, until you're skilled enough to use a real one.

## Training schedule

As a squire, my duties include waiting on my lord and his knights, serving them meals, looking after their horses, and keeping their armor and weapons clean. I've also been learning to handle different weapons, including swords and lances, on horseback and on foot. And there's still time for ball games and wrestling, to keep me fighting fit.

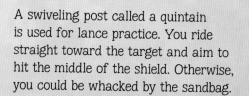

A swiveling post called a quintain is used for lance practice. You ride straight toward the target and aim to hit the middle of the shield. Otherwise, you could be whacked by the sandbag.

## How to be chivalrous

Proper behavior is as much part of being a knight as fighting skills. You have to follow a strict Code of **Chivalry,** which means you must . . .

**1** Be a loyal member of the Church

**2** Serve your lord with courage and loyalty

**3** Protect the weak and defenseless

**4** Be honest and always tell the truth

**5** Fight for the good of everyone

**6** Guard the honor of your fellow knights

**7** Never give up—see things through to the end

**8** Never turn your back on your enemy

# Life in the Castle

The earl's given me a day off from training, so let's go on a tour of Rhydding Castle. As you know, I've lived here since I was seven years old, so it feels like home.

The castle started off as a **manor house**, but it was attacked a couple of times. The earl's father had permission from the king to fortify it and make it safer, so he added a thick new wall and battlements, and now it's easier to defend.

The entrance to the main gatehouse has wooden doors and an iron-grilled gate called a portcullis. This can be lowered quickly to keep attackers out.

## Who lives here?

Apart from the knights, squires, and pages, lots of other people live in the castle. The most important are the lord and lady and their family, of course. Then there's the priest, steward (head servant), cook, butler, fletcher (arrow maker), carpenter, blacksmith, guards—and a host of servants.

The castle is surrounded by a thick stone wall with towers at regular intervals. Guards constantly patrol the walls. The battlements on top have squared openings that archers can fire through, then take cover. There are also arrow slits in the walls.

The castle bailey, the area within the castle walls, is always buzzing—traders selling goods, weapons being mended, and blacksmiths shoeing horses are just some of the many activities going on.

The keep is a tall stone tower where the lord and lady live. There's the great hall for feasts, the solar (the earl's bedroom), a dayroom for my lady, the garderobe (toilet), and the chamber I share with the other squires.

# "Arise, Sir Gilbert!"

There is no fixed age for becoming a knight. You'd usually be around twenty-one years old, but it depends on how your training goes and whether you (and your family) can afford to pay for your armor and warhorse.

At last! After all the training, the big day has arrived, and my lord has decided I am ready to become a knight. I had a long bath to wash away my sins. Then some of the other knights helped me get dressed in a red tunic, black stockings, and a red cloak. Afterward, I spent all night on my own, praying in the chapel.

This morning, they fixed on my spurs and strapped on my special sword belt. The earl gave me my own sword, and I knelt down in front of him and swore my **oath** of loyalty. He tapped me on each shoulder with his sword and said, "Arise, Sir Gilbert!"

## How to get knighted on the eve of battle

If you find the whole ceremony too long and imposing, try getting knighted before battle instead.

**1** The king asks if anyone wants to become a knight.

**2** You (and several others) step forward—it's a chance not to be missed.

**3** You swear a short oath and get a quick tap on the shoulder.

**4** That's it! Arise, Sir Knight!

In 1306, about three hundred men were knighted in Westminster Abbey, in London, England. Among them was the king's son, the future King Edward II. At a great feast afterward, two (fake) swans were brought in on a platter and the knights swore their oaths on the birds.

## The Black Prince

The eldest son of King Edward III, Prince Edward was a brilliant soldier and was knighted at the Battle of Crécy in 1346, when he was just sixteen years old. He was probably known as the Black Prince because of the color of his armor.

## William Wallace

Born in the 1270s, William became a hero in Scotland when he led a rebellion against Edward I and defeated the English at Stirling Bridge. He was made a Scottish knight in 1297, but Edward finally defeated his forces. The English pursued Wallace and took him prisoner. He was executed in 1305 and his head stuck on a spike on London Bridge.

# Arms and Armor

Now that I'm a full-fledged knight, I need to look the part. Battles (and tournaments) are dangerous, so it's vital to be well protected. A good suit of armor is essential. I've been to the armorer to have one made. (It cost me a fortune, but it fits really well— also essential.)

My steel-plate armor is strong and heavy, but it's surprisingly easy to move once you've got it on. It does get really hot, though, especially since I'm wearing a padded cap, jacket, and woolly leggings underneath. And the worst thing is that it's difficult to see when you're wearing your helmet.

Make sure you keep your armor in top condition by oiling and polishing it regularly. This will stop it from getting rusty—rusty armor's no use to anyone.

## Getting dressed

Putting on armor isn't easy, so give yourself plenty of time. Each piece needs to go on in the right order, starting with your sabatons (shoes) and finishing off with your great helm (helmet). You'll need your page or servant to help fasten all the buckles and tie all the laces.

## Armor parts

Each bit of your armor has a name that you'll need to know. After all, you don't want to go mixing up your cuisses (thigh guards) with your vambraces (arm guards), do you?

Great helm

Cuirasse

Aillettes

Couter

Vambrace

Gauntlet

Cuisse

Poleyn

Greave

Sabaton

## Weapons of war

Knights fight with a variety of weapons, including a lance and sword. Your sword is your most important weapon—it shouldn't be too heavy and must always be kept sharp.

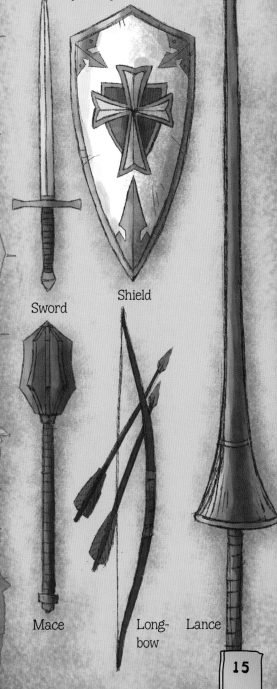

Sword

Shield

Mace

Long-bow

Lance

# Tournament Time

So, I'm all dressed up and ready to go, but there aren't any battles to fight at the moment. Instead, the earl's holding a tournament—it's my first, and I can't wait.

Tournaments are great for showing off your fighting skills and keeping your wits sharp. I'm pretty handy with a lance, so I've entered the jousting competition. I had to hang my shield up with the others—it's called "entering the **lists**." Anyway, the herald's just announced I'm on next. All right, helmet on, lance at the ready, and here goes. CHARGE!

## How to design your own coat of arms

Knights in full armor are tricky to tell apart, so you need a coat of arms. This gets passed down through your family, so everyone knows who you are and where you come from. There's a wide range of colors and designs to choose from, all with their own meanings. Add a stirring motto, too, if you like.

**WARNING!**

Be careful! Lances are dangerous weapons. Even though they're blunted, they can kill you or cause serious injury.

Helm

Mantle

Shield

MARSHALL

Surname

# How to win at jousting

Each bout of jousting lasts for three rounds, and points are awarded as follows:

**1 point** – for hitting your opponent on his body

**2 points** – for hitting him so hard your lance snaps

**3 points** – for knocking him off his horse

If the points are even, the winner may be decided by a sword fight on foot.

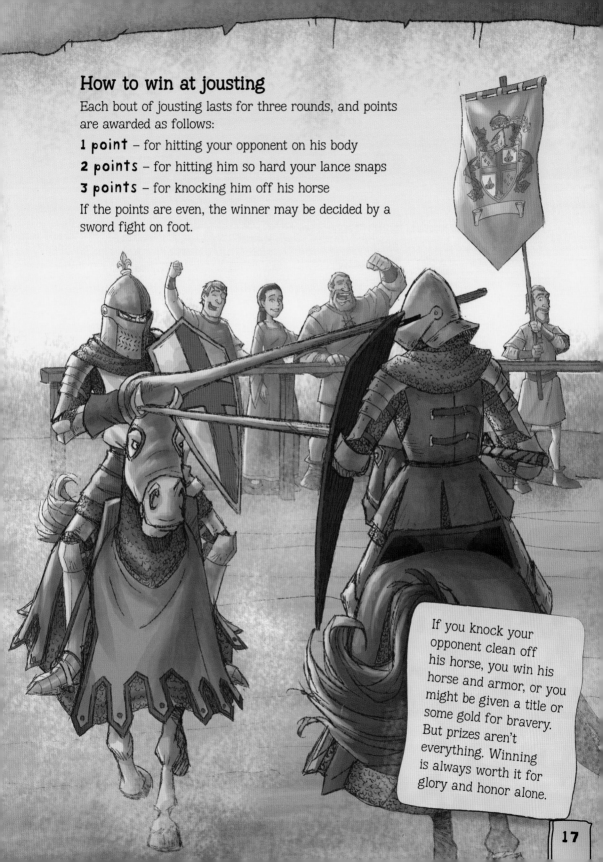

If you knock your opponent clean off his horse, you win his horse and armor, or you might be given a title or some gold for bravery. But prizes aren't everything. Winning is always worth it for glory and honor alone.

# Riding into Battle

Big news! We're heading off on campaign. The king's leading an army to fight the French, and the earl's busy **mustering** his troops to join him. It'll be my first taste of an actual battle—I just hope I can remember everything I've been taught.

It took days to get everything ready, and we finally set off. I'm traveling near the head of the troops with the earl. We've been riding for days now, and to tell the truth, it has been a real slog in the rain and mud. At night we pitch camp or take over some of the houses in the nearest village. The next morning we get up, feed and saddle the horses, grab breakfast, put on our armor, and ride off again.

Riding into battle makes you hungry, but don't expect top-notch grub. You'll most likely get some kind of potage (soup) and a hunk of coarse bread. If you're lucky. Armies usually loot food from the local peasants, taking their precious livestock and crops. There's wine or ale to drink, but never drink the water. (It'll make you sick.)

It's important that everyone knows their place and follows orders, so discipline is quite strict. It's part of your duty as a knight to make sure the rules are obeyed. Punishments range from fines for minor offenses to death for hitting your superior or sneaking secrets to the enemy.

## How to avoid the plague on the march

Bad news—you can't! Just keep an eye out for rats . . . The plague, or Black Death, is a terrifying disease that first hit England in the mid-fourteenth century. Victims develop a fever and large boils in their armpits. Most are dead by the next morning. Medieval doctors have no idea what caused it (spoiler alert: rats spread it), and there's no cure.

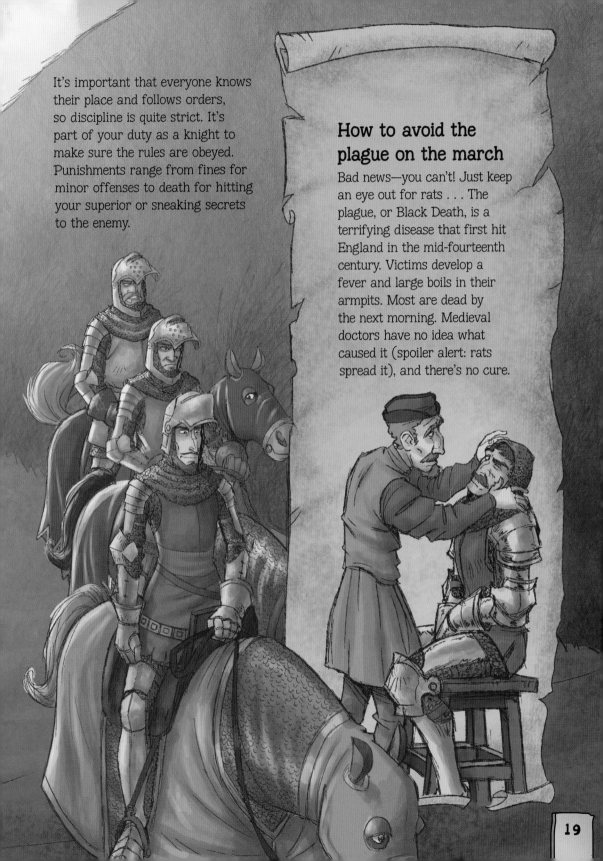

# Let Battle Begin!

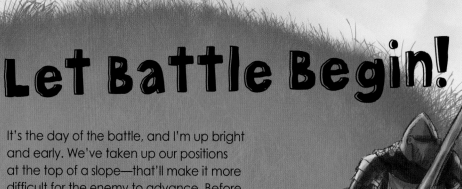

It's the day of the battle, and I'm up bright and early. We've taken up our positions at the top of a slope—that'll make it more difficult for the enemy to advance. Before we go in to fight, the earl gives us a pep talk to keep our spirits up. Then the signal is given and we gallop into action.

The first part of the battle is a **cavalry** charge. I'm riding my brand-new warhorse, Bayard. We all set off together, lances poised, and rush the enemy lines. Bayard behaves perfectly, but we come under attack from a tremendous hail of arrows. In the confusion, he rears up and I'm thrown to the ground . . .

## How to choose a warhorse

A top-notch warhorse can be very costly to buy and look after, so pick the right one. It needs to be big, brave, and powerful—the finest come from Italy or Spain. Make sure it's barded (well dressed) in a chanfron (head guard), mail coat, and cloth cover displaying your coat of arms. Then choose a warlike name.

At the Battle of Crécy in 1346, the English archers brought down charge after charge of French knights on horseback and won a crushing victory. Around four thousand French troops were killed.

# Hand-to-Hand Combat

I pick myself up and look around. I'm behind enemy lines, in the **mêlée**. The other knights have dismounted too, and we're getting ready to fight on foot with our swords. It's my first taste of hand-to-hand fighting.

It's chaos! The noise is terrible—men yelling and horses squealing. But all those years of sword-fighting practice are paying off. The French are no match for us, and we're pushing them back . . . we just need to stand our ground and pray that we come out of this alive. Wish I knew where Bayard is!

## How to survive a mêlée

Fighting in a mêlée is dangerous, however well-prepared you are. These tips could save your life:

**1** Stay close to your companions. If you're cut off, you'll be cut down.

**2** Don't get caught in the middle—you'll be trampled if there's a push from behind.

**3** Stay in one place and fight—moving in your armor will tire you out.

In a medieval battle, archers play a crucial part (especially in an English army). They fight with longbows, which are simple but deadly weapons. It takes years of practice to handle a bow well, and trained archers can fire hundreds of arrows a minute: a terrifying sight.

# Under Siege

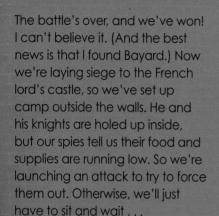

The battle's over, and we've won! I can't believe it. (And the best news is that I found Bayard.) Now we're laying siege to the French lord's castle, so we've set up camp outside the walls. He and his knights are holed up inside, but our spies tell us their food and supplies are running low. So we're launching an attack to try to force them out. Otherwise, we'll just have to sit and wait . . .

## How to defend a castle

If you're under attack, what can you do? Here are a few ideas . . .

**1** Pick off your attackers by firing arrows from the battlements and arrow slits. Then duck if they shoot back.

**2** Pour boiling oil from a murder hole (in the gateway ceiling) onto their heads. Ouch!

**3** Throw straw mats in front of their battering rams to protect the castle walls.

## Trebuchet

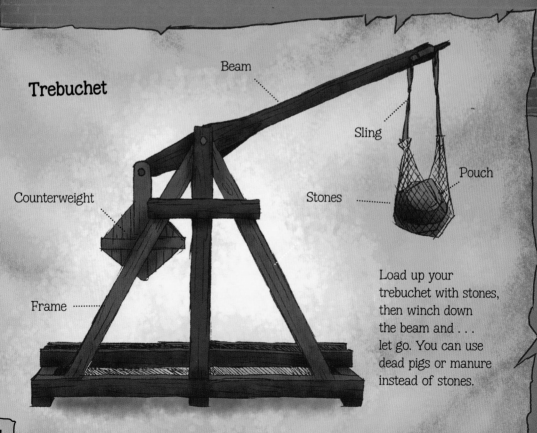

Beam

Sling

Pouch

Counterweight

Stones

Frame

Load up your trebuchet with stones, then winch down the beam and . . . let go. You can use dead pigs or manure instead of stones.

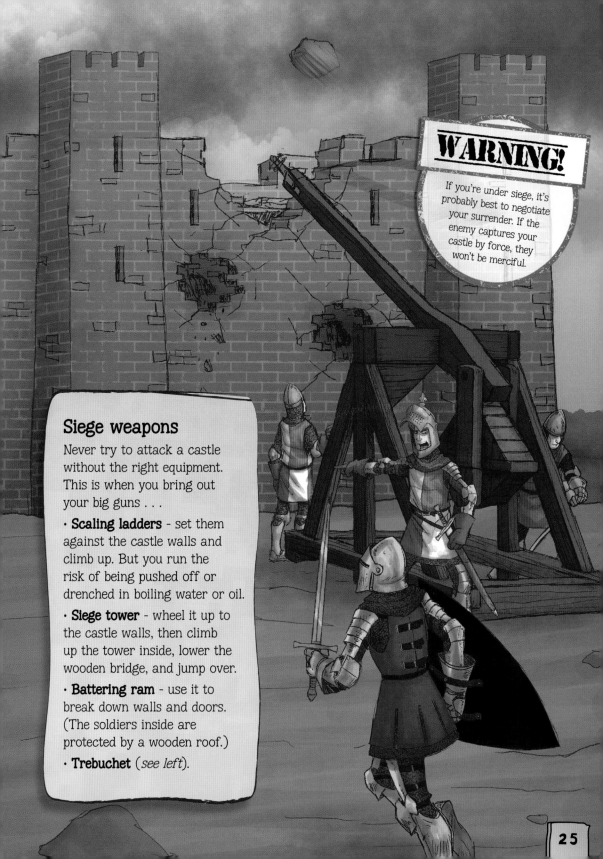

## WARNING!

If you're under siege, it's probably best to negotiate your surrender. If the enemy captures your castle by force, they won't be merciful.

## Siege weapons

Never try to attack a castle without the right equipment. This is when you bring out your big guns . . .

- **Scaling ladders** - set them against the castle walls and climb up. But you run the risk of being pushed off or drenched in boiling water or oil.

- **Siege tower** - wheel it up to the castle walls, then climb up the tower inside, lower the wooden bridge, and jump over.

- **Battering ram** - use it to break down walls and doors. (The soldiers inside are protected by a wooden roof.)

- **Trebuchet** (*see left*).

# Taken Prisoner

Just when things were going so well, disaster struck. We dug some tunnels underneath the castle walls, and the earl sent me to lead a secret **foray**. But I took a wrong turn and was captured, and now they've thrown me into this dungeon. It's cold and damp, and there are rats everywhere. Still, I won't be here for long. My captors demanded a ransom of 500 **florins** from the earl to let me go, and he's bound to pay up. Isn't he? I'm lucky, really. If I'd been a common soldier, the enemy wouldn't have kept me alive.

Getting a ransom paid can be tricky. Wars are costly, and there might not be much cash left in your lord's coffers. There are various places to go for help. Sometimes, the soldiers themselves will get together to raise the money, or the king might cover the cost.

According to the rules of chivalry, captured knights are sometimes kept in a comfortable castle room. For the ransom's sake, it's important to keep them healthy. After all, a prisoner's worth nothing dead.

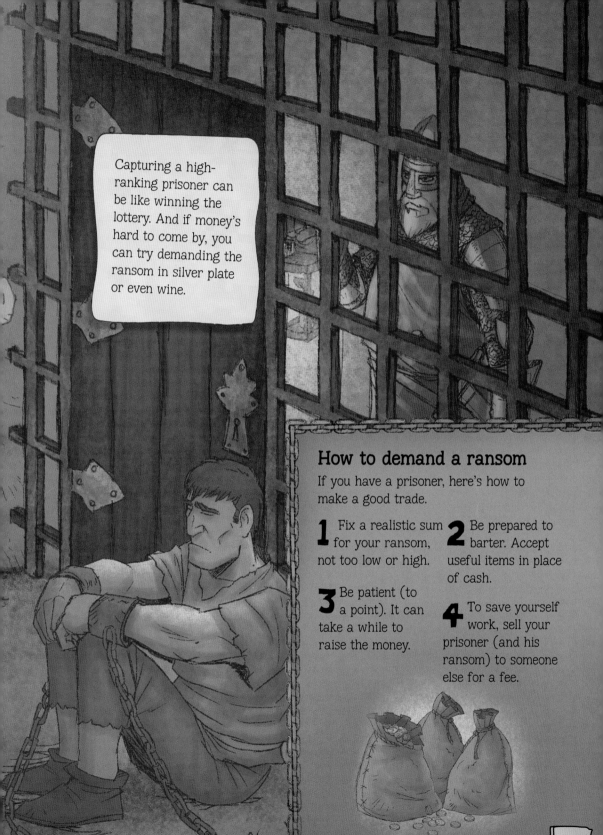

Capturing a high-ranking prisoner can be like winning the lottery. And if money's hard to come by, you can try demanding the ransom in silver plate or even wine.

## How to demand a ransom

If you have a prisoner, here's how to make a good trade.

**1** Fix a realistic sum for your ransom, not too low or high.

**2** Be prepared to barter. Accept useful items in place of cash.

**3** Be patient (to a point). It can take a while to raise the money.

**4** To save yourself work, sell your prisoner (and his ransom) to someone else for a fee.

# Victory Banquet

The lord always sits at the center of the high table because he's the most important person there. Everyone else sits in order of importance: the farther from the lord, the less important you are.

What a relief! The earl agreed to pay the ransom, and I was released. I knew he wouldn't just leave me to rot. Even better, he sent me a horse to ride home on—my faithful Bayard, of course.

Back home in Corfield Castle, we're having a great banquet to celebrate our victory. There's delicious food, plenty to drink, and excellent entertainment—the earl's definitely treating us. It might be my last feast here for a while. As a reward for my bravery, the earl's granted me some land of my own.

## Medieval kitchen

A feast can last for hours, with many different dishes, so the kitchen's kept busy. On the menu today there's roast suckling pig, roast peacock, venison pie, and eels in sauce, with sweet custard, jelly, marzipan, and eggs in pastry for dessert, all washed down with warm wine.

## How to be remembered

You're glad to be back in one piece, but you might not be so lucky next time. In case the worst happens, here's how to make sure people remember your knightly deeds:

**1** Give a good donation to the Church for Masses to be said when you're dead.

**2** Make plans for the grandest tomb you can afford, with a full-size effigy (image of you).

**3** Get someone to write a book about you, showing you in the best possible light.

A banquet can get messy. You eat with your fingers, or you use a knife and spoon. Instead of a plate, you have a trencher (a slice of stale bread). After the meal, the trenchers are given to the poor.

# Ten Fun Knight Facts

**1** Some knights went off to fight in the Crusades. These were wars between followers of Christianity and followers of Islam.

**2** Trainee knights gave each other piggyback rides to practice fighting on horseback.

**3** The wooden swords that knights used in training often weighed more than metal ones to build up the knights' upper-body strength.

**4** A disgraced knight had his spurs taken away and his shield hung upside down.

**5** At a tournament, ladies gave "favors"—scarves, veils, or sleeves—to their favorite knights.

**6** A jousting lance had a crown-shaped metal cap with three little blunted metal prongs.

**7** A servant called a kipper was sent to collect a knight's winnings at a tournament.

**8** Most knights owned two or three horses: a warhorse, a palfrey (for riding and hunting), and a packhorse.

**9** Some knights trained their warhorses to bite and kick on command—useful in battle.

**10** A knight's armor was a status symbol. The better the quality, the more important the knight.

# Glossary

**cavalry**
soldiers who fight on horseback

**chivalry**
rules of behavior that knights had to follow in battle and in life

**florin**
a gold coin used in Europe

**foray**
a sudden attack or raid into enemy territory

**lists**
a field near a castle where a tournament was held. "Entering the lists" meant competing in the tournament.

**manor house**
a large house, owned by a wealthy knight or lord

**mêlée**
disorganized combat fought at close range

**mustering**
gathering troops in preparation for a battle

**oath**
another word for a solemn promise

**page**
a young boy who serves a lord or knight in the hope of becoming a knight himself

**Renaissance**
a period of great learning in European history, from the early fourteenth to the late sixteenth century

**squire**
a boy in the second period of knightly training, after he has served as a page for seven years

# INDEX

## The Author

Anita Ganeri is an award-winning author of educational children's books. She has written on a huge variety of subjects, from Vikings to viruses and from Romans to world religions. She was born in India and now lives in England with her family and pets.

## The Artist

Mariano Epelbaum was born in Buenos Aires, Argentina. He grew up drawing and looking at small insects under the stones in the garden of his grandmother's house. He has worked as an art director and character designer for many films in Argentina and Spain.